HELICOPTERS

Valerie Bodden

CREATIVE ● EDUCATION

Published by Creative Education
P.O. Box 227, Mankato, Minnesota 56002
Creative Education is an imprint of The Creative Company
www.thecreativecompany.us

Design and production by Liddy Walseth
Art direction by Rita Marshall
Printed by Corporate Graphics in the United States of America

Photographs by Dreamstime (Bas Rabeling, Jvdwolf), Getty Images (Check Six, Ed Darack,
DreamPictures, MILpictures by Tom Weber, Time & Life Pictures), iStockphoto (Ken Babione,
Ross F. Bass, Sheila Broumley, Daniel Cooper, Chris Downie, FotoVoyager, Jean Frooms,
Jvdwolf, Stephen Meese, Tomas Pavelka, TCP)

Library of Congress Cataloging-in-Publication Data

Bodden, Valerie.
Helicopters / by Valerie Bodden.
p. cm. — (Built for battle)
Summary: A fundamental exploration of military helicopters, including their uses and carrying capacity,
history of development, rotors and other features, and famous models from around the world.
Includes bibliographical references and index.
ISBN 978-1-60818-127-8
1. Military helicopters—Juvenile literature. I. Title. II. Series.
UG1230.B63 2012
623.74'6047—dc22   2010054404

CPSIA: 030111 PO1447

First edition
2 4 6 8 9 7 5 3 1

BUILT for BATTLE

HELICOPTERS

Valerie Bodden

A loud *chop*, *chop*, *chop* sound fills the air.

Suddenly, a big vehicle rises straight up

into the sky and speeds away.

This is a military helicopter!

A helicopter is a flying vehicle with ROTORS. Military helicopters can be used to shoot tanks or other targets on the ground. They can fly soldiers or supplies from one place to another. Most military helicopters fly through the air at 100 to 200 miles (161-322 km) per hour.

A helicopter getting ready to pick up soldiers on a mountain

Famous Helicopter
UH-1 Iroquois

COUNTRY
United States
ENTERED SERVICE
1959
LENGTH
57 feet (17.4 m)
ROTOR LENGTH
48 feet (14.6 m)
WEIGHT
2.6 tons (2.3 t)
FASTEST SPEED
135 miles (217 km) per hour
CREW
1–4

The UH-1 was nicknamed the "Huey." It was built to carry soldiers into battle and fly injured soldiers to hospitals. The Huey was first made by the U.S. but is used by many other countries today.

Helicopters were first built in the 1940s. About 10 years later, helicopters with guns were used in war. The first helicopters flew slowly. Later, faster helicopters were built.

Most military helicopters are about 60 feet (18.3 m) long. The biggest helicopters can be more than 100 feet (30.5 m) long. That is longer than a basketball court!

All helicopters have a **COCKPIT** in the front.

Some helicopters also have an

open area called a cabin in the back.

The cabin has room for soldiers and supplies.

Attack helicopters do not have cabins.

They carry many weapons instead.

Mi-24 Hind

★ **Famous Helicopter** ★

COUNTRY

Soviet Union/Russia

ENTERED SERVICE

1976

LENGTH

57.4 feet (17.5 m)

ROTOR LENGTH

56.8 feet (17.3 m)

WEIGHT

9.4 tons (8.5 t)

FASTEST SPEED

208 miles (335 km) per hour

CREW

2

The Mi-24 is an attack helicopter with powerful weapons. But it also has a cabin that can carry up to eight soldiers into battle.

A helicopter's rotor can have two to eight blades. The blades spin to lift the helicopter. They can make the helicopter HOVER or fly forward, backward, or sideways! There is a small rotor on the helicopter's tail, too.

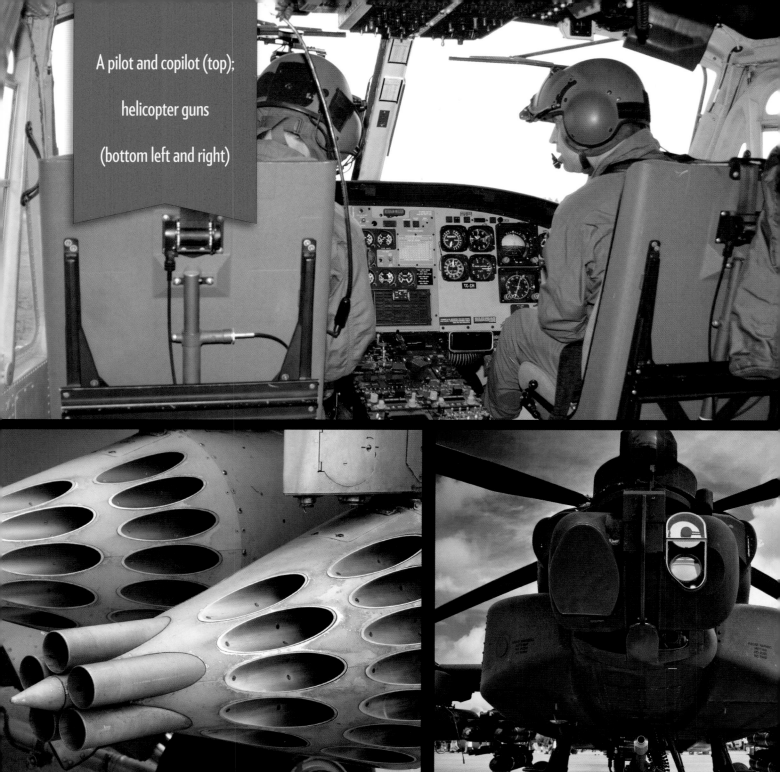

A pilot and copilot (top);

helicopter guns

(bottom left and right)

A pilot and copilot fly most helicopters. Some helicopters have other crew members, too.

A gunner fires a helicopter's weapons. A navigator tells the pilot where to go. Some helicopters have room for more than 50 soldiers in the cabin!

When an attack helicopter goes into battle, the pilot flies low to the ground. He might fly behind trees or hills to stay hidden from the enemy. When the helicopter gets to its target, the crew fires its weapons. They might fire AUTOMATIC CANNONS, guns, or MISSILES (*MIS-sulz*).

A military helicopter banking (turning) in the air during battle

AH64 Apache

COUNTRY

United States

ENTERED SERVICE

1984

LENGTH

58.2 feet (17.7 m)

ROTOR LENGTH

48 feet (14.6 m)

WEIGHT

5.7 tons (5.2 t)

FASTEST SPEED

182 miles (293 km) per hour

CREW

2

Apache helicopters are attack helicopters. They can fire at targets during the day, at night, or during bad weather. Their strong ARMOR can stop even the biggest bullets.

Most military helicopters have armor.

The armor stops enemy bullets from tearing

holes in the side of the helicopter. It keeps

the helicopter safe to fight another day!

GLOSSARY

armor—a layer of metal and other strong materials that covers a military vehicle and protects it from attack

automatic cannons—large guns that shoot many bullets very quickly

cockpit—the part of an airplane or helicopter where the pilot and other crew members sit

hover—to stay in one place in the air

missiles—exploding weapons that are pushed through the air by rockets to hit a target

rotors—machines that have blades that spin to make a helicopter fly

INDEX

WEB SITES

Royal Navy Interactive Tours: Lynx Helicopter
http://www.royalnavy.mod.uk/server/show/ConIpixGallery.4/changeNav/4714
Tour the inside of a military helicopter.

Super Coloring: Military Coloring Pages
http://www.supercoloring.com/pages/category/military/
Print and color pictures of all your favorite military machines.

READ MORE

David, Jack. *Apache Helicopters.* Minneapolis: Torque Books, 2008.

Demarest, Chris. *Alpha, Bravo, Charlie: The Military Alphabet.* New York: Margaret K. McElderry Books, 2005.